RPG Programming success in a day

Beginners' guide to fast, easy and efficient learning of RPG programming

Table Of Contents

Introduction

I want to thank you and congratulate you for purchasing the book, *"RPG Programming success in a day – Beginners' guide to fast, easy and efficient learning of RPG programming"*.

This book contains proven steps and strategies on how to make your first RPG.

You will learn how to make a logical story to make your game flow and incorporate exciting RPG elements to make sure that your first game is a hit among your first audience. You will also learn how to make use of exciting RPG techniques but still have the freedom to use variety when making up the rules of your game.

Thanks again for purchasing this book. I hope you enjoy it!

Chapter 1: The Magical World Of Role Playing Video Games

If you have always dreamed of making a game, creating your own role-playing game has probably crossed your mind. In order to be successful in creating this type of game, it is important to understand what sets this type of game apart from the rest.

What is an RPG?

As the name suggests, this is a type of game wherein players assume the roles of the playable characters within a particular fictional world. All the characters that one can play within such games are governed by a story line and a set of guidelines in order for the game to progress.

When you think about all the other types of video games that you have probably played (first person shooting games, strategy, action/adventure, simulation, arcade), you may think that all these games follow the same definition of what an RPG is. The lines have definitely begun to blur as technology evolves, but an RPG still has very special characteristics that are very different from the rest of the games available.

Nevertheless, it can be safely assumed that as long as you control a character in the story and the game attempts to immerse you in the game by letting you "experience" what your character is experiencing, then it is a role-playing game.

In most cases, RPG, genre-wise, is usually referred to JRPGs or Japanese Role Playing Games. JRPGs are usually single-player and are available mostly in gaming consoles. Despite being branded as a Japanese Role Playing Game, it does not necessarily mean that the game is made in Japan. A few examples of this type of RPGs are Final

Fantasy, Breath of Fire, Wild Arms, Suikoden, Tales of Destiny, Legend of Zelda, and Lufia.

On the other hand, most new people in gaming may refer to MMORPG when they say RPG. MMORPG or Massive Multiplayer Online Role Playing Game is a role-playing game that allows multiple people to play in one single game and story. Unlike typical RPGs, the story is not always the primary component that draws players to play. In most cases, some MMORPGs do not have any story at all. It is also common that the stories in MMORPGs have little effect and influence on the players' gaming experience and usually, the story is the least developed aspect.

RPG Traits

Most of the terms, game mechanics, and settings available in an RPG video game come from the early pen-and-paper forms like Dungeons and Dragons. Usually, a player would be able to control one or more characters and they would be able to finish the game by tackling different quests and reaching the end of a story line.

Most of the time, players in an RPG game explore an entire world and then solve problems or defeats enemies in order to progress in the game.

An RPG video game is also different from other games because the player is the one who establishes and develops how his or her character would turn out, and the game's difficulty is always based on how the created character would be able to surpass it. The game also does not force players to have extreme physical coordination or finish a scenario under a time limit, unless it is in the form of an action RPG.

What really makes an RPG special is that it is extremely dynamic — what would happen in the game is based on the player's decision on how he or she would play his or her chosen character. For this reason, many consider RPG as more intelligent and creative than the rest of the genres.

Are you ready to start creating your own RPG? First, you need to learn how to write and how it would progress.

Chapter 2: Common Elements in an RPG

Aside from the story and the characters, certain elements are included in games that make it easy for people to define that they are RPGs. A few of them are:

Leveling System

It is included in most RPGs to help prevent the stagnation of the game play. It is also an important feature that allows the player to control the difficulty of the game. Take note that the word "level" in the gaming world might mean a lot of things — usually, it refers to the progress of the game or locations within the game. In this case, "level" is referred to as character levels.

Typically, RPG characters start with low levels. Even if the story dictates that the characters you control in an RPG are the most powerful humans or entities in the world, they will always have low levels when you acquire them.

Character levels have multiple effects on the gameplay. The character's level influences its primary status or attributes. In some games, a character's level is a primary determiner or prerequisite of the skills it can use or learn.

Aside from that, other games give enemies levels, too. This mechanic can allow the game makers to create balance, provide scaling game difficulty, or just inform the player how tough the enemies are. For example, in Final Fantasy Tactics and Final Fantasy 8, the enemies' levels go up as well. Due to this, a weak enemy that can be defeated with two attacks early in the game might become stronger too as your characters level up.

Experience Points

Together with levels, experience points or simply "experience" exists in RPGs. Experience points are rewarded to characters whenever they accomplish something within the game. In classics, experience points can be gained by defeating monsters and enemies.

Whenever a character gains a specific amount of experience points, it will level up — usually, in increments of 1. As a character's level goes up, it is the norm that the required number of experience points goes up as well. For example, a level 2 character may require 300 experience points to go up to level 3. When he reaches level 3, the game will require him 400 experience points to get to the next level. The gradual increase in the experience point requirement may be linear or logarithmic.

Status Attributes

In RPGs, characters have status attributes that define how well they perform in the game. The most important attribute present in most RPGs is health or HP (Health Points). Health points determine how much damage a character can take before it dies, become unconscious, or the game ends.

Aside from HP, a few of the most common status attributes that you can find in RPGs are attack points (offense, physical attack damage, power, strength) and defense points (defense, damage reduction, vitality, endurance). Attack points determine the amount of damage you can do to an enemy's HP — yes, enemies have status attributes, too. On the other hand, defense points reduce the amount of damage an enemy can do to your character's HP.

The game developer may add other status attributes to spice up the game, make the players more immersed, introduce creative battle and gaming concepts, and incorporate higher levels of strategic thinking. For example, for medieval and magical RPGs, MP or magical points may be used. MP limits the number of special or magical attacks that a character can do.

Battles

The battle system is one of the core components of RPGs. The battle system separates an RPG from a visual novel. Battles have various uses in an RPG. It can be used to keep your players busy and forget the story for the meantime. It can also be used as a primary method of gaining levels for your characters. It can be used as a plot point in the story. A good example of that is a boss battle, wherein your protagonists battles with the current or main antagonist.

Battles can be executed in multiple ways in a game. In classic RPGs, battles are usually executed through random forced encounters while some are timer-based and/or based on the number of steps the player has made in the game.

On the other hand, newer RPGs have taken away the concept of forced battles and have given players the chance to decide if they want to battle or not. For example, in Lunar, enemies are shown in the field. If the player touches or interacts with them, a battle will start. The player can choose to avoid the monsters to prevent battles.

Battle System

Different battle systems have been developed over the years. Changes in battle systems were created in order to add more immersion and enjoyment to the sometimes dreadful battles. A few of the most common battle systems are:

1. Traditional Turn Based or TTB

Each character and enemy in the battlefield gets a turn in performing an action. The turns of each character is based on agility or any status attributes that governs the speed of the character. Traditional turn based system can be in the form of setting the actions of the whole party first and then executing it once the actions are predetermined. Each character and enemy get to perform one action every turn. A good example of this system is Wild Arms 1 and Suikoden II.

2. Per Character Turn Based or PCTB and Conditional Turn Based or CTB

Another form of a turn-based system is that actions will be set individually and once the player confirms the action, the character will immediately perform it. This has two forms. The first one is PCTB. The second one is CTB.

However, unlike PCTB that only allows one action per character per whole turn, CTB allows faster characters to have multiple turns. A game that uses this type is Final Fantasy X.

3. Active Time Battle or ATB

Active turn battle or ATB was popularized by the Final Fantasy series and it was created by most of the series' franchises' game designer, Hiroyuki Ito. Instead of just going through turns, each character has a timer or gauge that fills up. The speed of the gauge depends on the agility stat that governs the turn speed of the character. When the gauge is full, the character can execute an action. The gauge will then empty itself after that.

There are two modes of active time battle. The first one is Active. The second one is Wait. Wait mode allows the users to take time in deciding the action of the character. While deciding, the gauge of other characters and enemies will stop. On the other hand, Active mode allows faster battles. Even if the player is deciding on what action to do, the gauges of other characters will continue to fill up. It allows monsters to act out as soon as their gauge fills up.

4. Real Time Battle or RTB

RTB has been the dominant battle system type in modern RPGs. It induces more action and requires a lot of player attention and control. This type stimulates the player to use most of the gaming skills that he or she has — reflexes, strategic thinking, and hand-to-eye coordination, among others.

RTB allows a player to move freely on the battlefield and take action whenever he or she wants. In some cases, "cooldowns" are implemented to add challenge and balance to the game. For example, in Tales of Destiny, using items in battles has a cooldown period.

Items

Generally, there are two types of items in RPGs. The first type is consumables. The second type is key items. Consumables are items that can be used to aid the characters survive the game world. Examples of this type are potions that can be used to recover a character's HP or grenades that can be used to damage enemies.

Key items are used to get through certain events and plot points in the game. For example, a key to a certain door is a key item.

Items can be acquired by buying them from NPC merchants, getting them from treasure chests, or looting them from monsters.

Equipment

Equipment or battle gears are items that your character can wear to increase their stats or let them gain special abilities. In simple RPGs, battle gears usually consist of weapons, armors, and accessories. Some RPGs can be complex about battle gears. They might have weapons, shields, body armor, leg armor, headgear, and accessories.

NPCs or Non-Playable Characters

Your characters are your playable characters. Anyone aside from them is considered a non-playable character. They have many uses in RPGs. They can be used as plot devices, merchants, information source, or decorations with the only purpose of making a town or a location in the game appear lively.

Chapter 3: Game Elements and Development

Developing an RPG or any game alone does not only involve a storywriter and a programmer. It is true that nowadays, a team of two people or even a lone individual can create a decent RPG or even an RPG that can rival classics.

However, that is not always the case. Creating an RPG or a game requires a lot of skills. Writing and programming are not enough. If those two are the only skills that you have, it is required that you compensate with incredible amounts of creativity or a decent amount of money if you want a sellable game. You can also just learn those other skills, but it will take some time.

As mentioned, a role-playing game is not just story and code. It can be done, true. But if you want to have a decent RPG, then you must go beyond story and code. You must not limit yourself to that. If you have ever seen an end game credits for an RPG or any game, you will know that developing a game requires more than two or three people.

You need to create a team that will provide you with the other skills that you do not have. You can invite friends that can help you. Alternatively, you can scour the Internet for RPG development communities or other communities to get assistance.

So what are those skills that you need, anyway? Well, it can be summed up into two categories. First is graphics. Second is sounds. And if you want to have an idea what skills or people you need to get the job done, read the following.

Graphics

When it comes to games, graphics are essential. They are one of the main components that will immerse and attract your players. It is the first thing that your players will experience and criticize. The story will come later. The battle system will happen later.

However, never forget that good graphics can only get you buyers. Good story and gaming experience will get you followers. As long as your game's graphics are not disgustingly horrible, it will pass as a decent game.

The less complex your gameplay is, the easier the demands for graphics would be. Usually, the interface is the marriage of technology and the guidelines of the game. Apart from deciding how your game would generally look like, you would also need to consider what the player would see onscreen in order to make your game guidelines work. The look of the game would also decide what kind of players would be attracted into playing your game.

For example, a card game type of RPG allows great control of your guidelines and it makes it possible for the player to be reminded of all the explanations that you have mentioned early in the game. However, it makes the game visually look less dynamic since players are not able to see the action taken by the character. However, this may appeal to players that are more narrative-driven and are fine with text since they can imagine what is going on anyway. You can also choose to create a game in side-scrolling 2D if you want your game to have the elements of action/adventure games.

There are four types of "graphic modes" in games, and they are:

Text-Based Graphics

Most of the old WRPGs or Western Role Playing Games in personal computers started with text-based graphics. One of the most successful text-based RPGs is MUD 2 (Multi User Dungeon 2). In addition to being a decent RPG during its time, it can be considered as the oldest MMORPG in the world. However, Avalon is the pioneer since it has properly defined what an MMORPG is. It was the first that created the features and the standards that most MMORPGs nowadays follow.

With text-based graphics, it is possible to pull off a game that only requires a writer and a programmer. However, only a few people yearn for this type of RPG. Also, you will be required to make up for the missing common elements with your story and gaming system.

2D Graphics

Despite 2D RPG games being mostly popular two decades ago, it is still the standard, especially for indie role-playing game developers. With a 2D RPG, you will require graphic artists. Mainly, you need two types of artists. First, you need a sprites artist. Sprites are images that can be animated — though not all sprites need to be animated for a game. You need sprites for your character, enemies, and NPCs.

Second, you need a background image artist. Background images provide the "world" where your sprites will roam around. In a game, there are two ways to create a background for your sprite. First, you can use a still background. The world will be painted, and you will just need to place collision boxes or lines to prevent your sprites from wandering off to places they should not be. An example of a game that used still backgrounds is Star Ocean 2. Using still backgrounds can be quite expensive and time-consuming, especially if your game has a lot of locations.

Second, you can use tilesets. Tilesets are image files filled with small images that can be used as tiles in a game. They can be used to create fixed backgrounds where your characters can move around. Think of it like placing Lego pieces to create a map. This method is cheaper and less taxing for the artist. Tilesets are reusable and your creativity is limitless with them.

Also, the responsibility of the designs of the maps or world will depend on the programmer, or a designated mapmaker in your team. Most old 2D RPGs use tilesets. One of the most notable RPGs that use this type of background-ing is Pokemon.

Other responsibilities of background artists are to provide parallax backgrounds and create foregrounds. They can be also tasked with creating in-game menus, dialogue boxes, logos, and even cut-scene images. Foregrounds and parallax backgrounds are not necessarily needed, but they provide more depth to your game world. Also, with the correct usage of parallax backgrounds, you can achieve a 3D or 2.5D feel in your game.

2.5 Graphics

Two and a half dimensional graphics, or most commonly referred to as 2.5D, is the method of using 2D graphics to appear 3D. However, when it comes to video games in general, 2.5D might mean a few things. A 2.5D game might be a game that uses 2D graphics to achieve pseudo 3D; uses both 2D and 3D graphics; or uses 3D graphics mainly, but the game's camera only emphasizes two dimensions. In RPGs, the first two definitions are commonly used — the third one is usually reserved for platformer games.

The first definition, using 2D to achieve pseudo 3D, can be achieved by creating isometric sprites, backgrounds, and maps. Instead of the usual oblique view or 2D-ish view, isometric sprites create an illusion that the player is viewing the game in an isometric view (one that lets people see three dimensions).

The second definition, using 2D and 3D, has been the most popular choice when it comes to 2.5D. Usually, the world is rendered in 3D and the characters and other objects in the world are 2D sprites. A good example of a game in 2.5D graphics is Azure Dreams.

On the other hand, in some cases, both techniques are employed. A good example that did such is Breath of Fire 3.

3D Graphics

You might be more familiar with 3D graphics. There are pros and cons with a 3D title. First of all, it will require a huge initial investment. Creating a 3D world is a time-consuming process. Beautifying that world is another story.

Of course, the time you spend will depend on how much complexity you put in your 3D graphics. To be precise, the number of polygons of your 3D models dictate how much time that you will spend. In addition, you must also take into account the machine of the user. Although, with simple 3D RPG games, you do not need to worry about that.

Also, 3D artists are a bit pricy. On the other hand, when creating a 3D game, it does not mean that you are spared from hiring a graphic artist. Do note that your 3D models and environment will require bitmap images. On a different note, if you do everything by yourself, 3D computer graphic software applications are also expensive. However, you can settle for free ones such as Blender.

With 3D, take note that coding may become more complex. In 2D and 2.5D games, you will be dealing with simple coordinates (x and y). With 3D, you will need to deal with 3 dimensions (x, y, and z). When dealing with collision and position, 3D will give you a greater challenge.

Sounds

Another core component of games is sound. In the sound department, you need two things. First is background music, and second is sound effects. In case that you want to add more depth to your game's sound department, you might want to get some ambient sounds, too.

Sound is probably one of the most basic components that should be available in every game, yet most starting developers neglect paying attention to it. The background music (BGM) plays a very important role in setting the tone of every location and action that you have created in the game. The sound effects (SFX) also make the movements of the character declared to all players and also work to make a fictional world feel more natural to any player.

Of course, you will need a music composer and a sound effect person to get the right feel for your game. With sound effects, you can get away with this easier. Luckily, most developers have access to libraries of BGM and SFX online, which are already categorized according to genres. Most of them provide free samples that you can use in your game. Of course, make sure that you do credit them and understand your resource's terms and agreement with its samples.

On the other hand, if you want to create unique libraries for your games to distinguish your game from any homebrewed RPG out there, then you can record or create your own. All you need is a recording device and any digital audio workstation (DAW).

If you are not a tight budget, you can get Audacity. It is a free DAW that you can use. However, it is not as powerful or as easy to use as commercial audio workstations. It can be, but you need to learn more about music production and a bit of programming to make full use of Audacity's potential and power.

You can render all sound files as .wav to make sure that the sound would not need to be trimmed and would instantly play after a trigger. An MP3-formatted sound has silence at the beginning of the track, so you would not want to use that format when rendering sound effects and music.

However, do note that using .wav files can pose a huge drawback. That drawback is that .wav file sizes are quite big. A minute of BGM will cost you around 50MB or more, depending on the quality of the .wav file you will use. Just imagine: If you have 10 towns with different BGMs, you will instantly make your players download a game that will take up 500MB or more. A huge chunk of your game's file size is spent on audio alone. Some players will not appreciate that unless the sounds of your files are worth it.

By the way, the quality and size of the .wav file are determined by the file or recording's bit-rate, sample rate, and if it is in mono or stereo.

On the other hand, the gap silence padding at the beginning of an MP3 file, which is caused by decoders, is usually around 0.05ms long. So, when it comes to sound effects, the short delay is unnoticeable. If you want to use it in music, you have to be smart with the composition. You can put an intended silence at the beginning and ending of your songs. You can use a simple fade-in and fade-out trick.

In case that you want to achieve gapless playback and smaller audio files, you can use .ogg instead. However, some RPG or game development kits do not support this file type.

If you are aiming for a high quality RPG with a heavy plot, you will need voice actors. Nowadays, voice acting is standard when it comes to RPGs. Nevertheless, you can get away without it if you are just creating a small indie project. Nevertheless, it might be advisable to provide little voiced lines in your game. Adding at least voiced grunts during battles does make a difference in the quality of your game.

Miscellaneous

Other than the graphics and sounds, you must also think about localization and marketing if you are dead serious in creating an RPG that will sell. You will need translators for your game. Also, you will need people to market it. Of course, you can also handle the marketing part. If you just want to create a game, you can just ignore this section.

Aside from that, you will need a director and a producer. If you are both the writer and the programmer, you will be the perfect fit as the producer and the director.

Chapter 4: Platform and Development Kits

Now that you have your storyline, you can move on to the more technical aspects of your game.

Creating an RPG would not really demand that you know how to code, but knowing how would give you a huge advantage when you want to make use of better interface, or a more complex set of controls and sound.

Also, knowledge on programming will allow you to develop your game easier. The knowledge of conditions, variables, operations, loops, et cetera, will help you create a much richer game faster. In addition, using a development kit or integrated development environment in creating games will be much easier since you will be more familiar with how things work.

You may opt to use available RPG maker tools (which would be discussed in a later chapter) to make it easy for you and cut down on development time and create maps and characters right away. However, the list that is going to be discussed here would give you a better idea on how you can improve the next games that you would be creating and to create better atmospheres for the game that you are trying to create now.

In order to know what software you are going to use to create your RPG, you have to consider the gaming platform that you want to target.

Platform

When creating your game, always think of what hardware is going to be used by the player to play your game. Arguably, a PC platform makes any game more accessible to your audience, and can also set expectations about the simplicity or complexity of the game. If you are going to use other consoles, you will, of course, set other expectations. For example, developing a game for XBOX would naturally make your audience look for better graphics and sound.

However, do not be discouraged. Do not push yourself too much. Despite what many believe, graphics is not everything. Despite being the core aspect that most gamers criticize, you do not need to worry about not reaching the graphical complexity of most modern games. Remember, Minecraft became successful. It is not the fanciest thing on Earth, graphics wise. And it was able to make it on XBOX.

In addition, the gaming market has been saturated with eye candy games that bring nothing to the table. In RPG, it is usually about the content — the story. After that, the game system follows. Also, the current market leans toward "indie pixel graphics." So, again, if you can export it to XBOX or other high-end consoles, why not?

Development Kits and Environments

Contrary to popular belief, creating an RPG does not require that you start learning how to code. There are various online and offline tools that would enable you to create a working RPG without knowing much about programming — all you need to do is to fill up the blanks in forms, and voilà, you have a working game.

However, while creating an RPG is now easier and less technical, it does not mean that creating such a game is easy and for everyone. It takes a lot of preparation and intense creativity to make an interesting game.

Since you are about to program and launch your homebrew project, here are some of the game development kits and environments that you can use in order to create the RPG game you want.

RPG Maker

For beginners and hobbyists, this is the most ideal game development application that you can use to create your RPG. If you have minimal programming to no coding experience, RPG Maker can help you create a decent RPG.

This RPG development platform creates classic 2D RPGs that are similar to the popular SNES RPGs. In the newer versions, battle scenes can be set to 2.5D. And with some tweaking, you can turn your your whole game into 2.5D.

No coding is required with this program, but minimal knowledge in programming flow is a bit needed. It contains resources such as sprites, tilesets, background images, BGMs, sound effects, and animations that you can use to develop your game. So, you can create a game with this alone.

Fun fact: RPG Maker is a series of RPG development applications created by Enterbrain, a Japanese game and magazine publishing company. As of now, the latest version of RPG Maker is RPG Maker VX Ace. Getting the program costs around S70, which is relatively cheap compared to other game-making engines and platforms. You can instantly get the program from Steam or get it from RPG Maker's website. Alternatively, you can try out the trial version for 30 days and see if it is the right platform for you.

A few of the celebrated features of RPG Maker are:

1. Simple map editing and creation – Just place the tilesets on a mapsheet and you are done.

2. Instant dungeon generator

3. Simple Character, Enemy, Skill, Item, and Equipment manager and database

4. Character generator – This allows the creation of custom character sprites and portraits within a few clicks.

5. High quality resource packs

Those are just a few of the features that will benefit you.

However, there are a few cons that this platform has. Most of those cons might be a problem for advanced users and ambitious new game developers.

For one, you will be restricted to JRPG style or RPG Maker's definition of RPG. There is little room for customization in RPG Maker, especially when it comes to the RPG Maker's game engine.

However, extensive customization is still possible, but you will need to learn Ruby and RGSS 3 (Ruby Game Scripting System). Another workaround to that is to get user-created scripts and embed it into your game. On the other hand, your game will be limited to PCs only.

The troubles might not be worth it, especially if you are an ambitious beginner and want to have a unique RPG. It will be much better to try a different programming platform if that is the case. Nevertheless, if you want a good introduction to RPG development, this is a good program to try.

Game Maker Studio

This software boasts of cutting development time by 80%. It works by either dragging and dropping elements into the interface or by using its built-in scripting language. It is great for creating apps for iOS, Android, Windows, or HTML5 game browsers if you want to put your game online. Unfortunately, this software is only great for single-player games, but it's starting to develop into making multiplayer games possible in the near future.

Technically, Game Maker Studio is free. However, you will be limited to creating games for computers that run on Windows only.

If you want to port your game into different consoles and platforms such as Mac OS X, Ubuntu, Android, HTML5, iOS, and Windows Phone 8, you will need to get the Master edition, which will cost you around $800.

To be honest, the cost is too high. However, it is justifiable due to the restrictions that some companies such as Apple impose to the developers of Game Maker. Also, the return of investment in having a game on the Android and iOS market alone is high. Just imagine putting your app on the market and selling it for $1 each, and you will be able to get the money you spent with Game Maker if at least 800 people test your app.

On the other hand, if you just want to unlock the full capabilities of Game Maker Studio, you will need to get the Professional version, which costs around $500. It allows team development and other services from YoYoGames, the company that partnered with Mark Overmars to develop and improve Game Maker.

When it comes to game development, Game Maker Studio is capable of the development of different types of games. It can be used to develop platformers, first person shooters, visual novels, point and click games, and RPGs.

Just like RPG Maker, Game Maker Studio is designed to make game development easier and friendlier to newcomers in the industry. Little programming and coding experience are needed in order to create a game in Game Maker. What's more, Game Maker is capable of making 3D games.

However, Game Maker Studio does not come with resources intended for RPGs. So in this case, you might need team members in order to make a complete and decent RPG.

On a different note, lack of knowledge in the internal structures of games and RPGs will hinder a complete beginner to create an RPG with Game Maker. Despite it being user-friendly and all, it is still up to the programmer or user to develop a program of his own. Unlike RPG Maker, there are no presets or predefined RPG engines in Game Maker. You will be forced to create one from scratch.

Even with that setback, there is a simple workaround that you can use. Primarily, you can use open source RPG game engines made in Game Maker by community members. With those engines, you can study how advanced programmers develop their own RPGs. On the other hand, you can just use the engine and put your content in it.

In addition, do note that you will need to learn Game Maker's GML (Game Maker Language). If you have prior programming experience, the syntax and the environment of GML is similar to C, C++, and Java. However, keep in mind that even if GML is similar to those languages, GML is not an object-oriented language. So, expect that you cannot create classes. Though, you can create pseudo classes with Game Maker's objects, but that is another lesson to tell.

The greatest strength of Game Maker lies within its user-friendliness and versatility. If you are ambitious, want a unique game, and have grand plans with your project, you can choose Game Maker Studio. Be reminded that the learning curve can be steep. But compared to other development kits, this is a much easier option.

It is also a great way to learn how to code right away if you want to create your game from scratch on your own using the software's scripting language. You can watch demos on how to do that, or you can ask the community for advice and suggestions on how you can code your first game.

Like most software, the more demanding the features you demand for your game, the more expensive it is going to be. Right now, try the free edition.

Sploder

This is a web-based RPG game creation tool that you can use to get your game started in no time at all. It also allows you to make use of its Graphic Editor tool if you want to create your own art. This is probably the easiest tool that you can use to create a game and use great art too, since all you need is to drag and drop the assets that you want.

Despite its simplicity, you would still be able to create layers and layers of dungeons here, and add all the elements that you want in your game. All you need is to create an account to save your game. If you want to create a game without having to learn how to code or script, this is the software for you.

However, do note that Sploder is too limited and its primary purpose should be introducing you to game development. It is not actually intended to create RPGs. Although you can make one with it, it will not be rich as a regular RPG in the market.

Construct 2

This is another HTML5 game engine that allows you to drag and drop. This is probably the best tool that you can use if you want to rapidly develop a 2D game from scratch. All you need is to drag and drop elements into a level, then specify the events and behaviors that you want to incorporate there. This is also a great tool to test prototypes of game ideas that you have on mind.

A single project can also be launched for different platforms. You can instantly launch your game for the Web and Facebook, or use wrappers for PC, iOS, Android, Mac, and Linux after you are done programming your game.

Construct 2 is similar to Game Maker Studio. However, Game Maker has a few advantages over Construct 2. First of all, the free version of Game Maker has no limitations. The free version of Construct 2 limits users with 100 events, 4 layers, and 2 special effects. With game Maker, you get full functionality without limits sans the professional features.

Another advantage of Game Maker versus Construct 2 is that Game Maker can handle big projects without significant performance issues. Although GML is not optimized for best performance, you just need to optimize your code. When it comes to Construct 2, the larger your project, the larger frames per second reduction it gets.

Of course, Construct 2 has its own edges against Game Maker Studio. First of all, it can take advantage of JavaScript. Since Construct 2 is an HTML5 maker, anybody who has a background in web development and client side scripting can easily master Construct 2. Compared to GML, JavaScript is a much better language.

Another advantage is that Construct 2 focuses on HTML5. HTML5 is slowly seizing control of the Internet. It has been proven that web-based games are popular and profitable, thanks to Flash. But since HTML5 is taking over Flash, HTML5 games seem to be a profitable choice. However, Game Maker games can be exported, too, but you will need to get the Professional version and upgrade it to allow HTML5 porting, which will cost you around $350.

Also, Construct 2 is cheaper than Game Maker Studio when it comes to opening the export and porting features. The Personal License for Construct 2 costs around $130. However, there is a minor setback. As of now, Construct 2 cannot port to Linux, Mac OS X, and Windows. Those features will be available on Construct 3.

Lastly, if the game you made with Construct 2 exceeds $5,000 in profits, you will be forced to upgrade to Business License, which might cost you around $300 to $450. In Game Maker, there are no commercial limitations even if your copy of the software is free.

Unity3D

Meet one of the favorites of the indie developer community — Unity. This engine allows you to create games for the following platforms: XBOX, PS3, Android, Mac, Windows, Wii U, and of course, the Web.

Developing a game using this platform is very similar to Construct2 — the difference is that a level is called a scene, and scenes contain game objects. Each object that you are going to use would contain scripts. Scripts are often written using the UnityScript, Boo, or C++.

To be honest, it is not recommended for beginners to jump on Unity right away. Despite being usable and free, the learning curve will be steeper. It is advisable that you start with RPG Maker. Learn the basic concepts of RPG making, and then familiarize yourself with a bit of coding using Sploder. After that, try to create an RPG engine of your own in Game Maker or Construct 2. Familiarize yourself with how you can program with GML or JavaScript.

In Unity 3D, you can also use JavaScript, so it will not be a waste of time and effort to learn it. Once you get full understanding of how to create an RPG from scratch, then it will be the best time to learn Unity 3D.

Also, learning and mastering Unity 3D or even Unreal, which will be discussed next, will require a lot of time. It will be a big investment. And do not expect that you will be able to create a game instantly. You will just be frustrated.

On the other hand, if you are that decided and you do not know how to code, don't fret. The Unity has an Asset Store, where you can purchase scripts, animations, and other assets that you want to incorporate in your game. Doing so would quickly ensure that all the elements would be working, and so that you do not have to reinvent the wheel each time you decide to use this engine to create a game.

Unreal Development Kit

Unreal Development Kit or UDK is a favorite tool for first person action games, but it can be modified to create an RPG. It is a full game development kit, and may be tough for beginners to use, but it is definitely worth looking into if you want to create a great-looking first-person RPG. If that is your goal for your first game, you would want to check out the tutorials on how to make use of C++ in this engine, and code scripts using the engine's built-in UnrealScript to generate in-game behaviors.

Be reminded that Unreal can only create 3D games. It is essential that you either get a team or learn how to create 3D models when you try Unreal.

Now that you have the content of your game ready and you have a clear idea of how the game would look and feel like on your choice of console, it's time to whip out the computer and get into production.

Chapter 5: Creating the Story

Since you are considering programming an RPG, you need to pay attention to how the story would progress. In a game like RPG, the internal logic of the game is extremely important. It has to follow a strict set of guidelines in order for it to be playable and programmable. How the game is written dictates the sets of logic that would be available in the game.

But of course, you do not need to limit yourself. If you will be the writer for your RPG, then write as you will. The story you will create will determine the quality of your game. You can set aside the logic first. Just create a story that you are familiar with.

However, make sure that you do your research. On the other hand, do not worry about the length of your story or your game. The most important thing is that you complete your story. Once that is done, then you can proceed on thinking how you can insert it on your game.

Creating a Strong RPG Story

A good RPG resembles real life — the smaller goals of the characters may change from time to time, depending on the choices that the player has chosen, but it follows a main story that ends with an achievement of a single goal. By doing so, the character created for the game becomes established and dynamic at the same time by following a storyline with a well-defined ending.

To be honest, writing a story for an RPG is a lot like writing a novel or a screenplay. If you have noticed or have played some RPGs before, some RPGs are formatted like a book. A good example is Valkyrie Profile.

The story of Valkyrie Profile was neatly separated in eight chapters. Screenplays are usually divided in eight sequences, too. Of course, it is not a rule set in stone. But it is a formula that works smoothly.

The eight sequences in the screenplay are:

1. Citing the Status Quo and Starting the Initial Incident

    The status quo of the protagonists is explored. And a certain incident whether big or small will break that status quo. For example, the hero lives a peaceful life. And then he find himself in the middle of a huge crime in the kingdom.

2. Predicament Is Discussed and the Protagonists Get Locked in in It

The kingdom captures the hero. He was innocent. In order to prove his innocence, he must do something for the King. He must kill the evil dragon who infests the continent. If he declines, he will be sentenced to death. The hero chooses to kill the dragon instead since he has been literally left with no choice.

3. Protagonists Meets the First Obstacle and the Stakes Get Higher

The hero journeys to the lair of the dragon. He meets an evil man. He was the one actually controlling the dragon. There are more dragons on his base and he plans to wipe out the kingdom. The only one who knows about his plan is him. He decides to destroy the dragon and kill the evil man. He tried to do that, but the man escaped. He was left with the dragon. He killed the dragon.

4. Midpoint of the Story

The hero returns to the kingdom to report the death of the dragon and the evil man. The king was grateful and his innocence was proven. Since he was able to kill the dragon, he was appointed as the kingdom's champion. The king tasked him to end the reign of the evil man.

5. Exploration of a Sub Plot and Rise of Conflict

The hero meets some friends and party members during his journey. He meets one of the evil mans lackeys — a mini boss. The lackey made the hero's life difficult.

6. Conflict Ends and the Sub Plot Ends

The hero and his friends defeated the lackey. He was now in front of the evil man's lair.

7. A New Problem that Caused by a Twist

The hero and the evil man met. The evil man told him a secret. The hero was actually the son of the evil man. The evil man was actually the good guy. He just wanted to take revenge on the king. The hero was confused on what to believe in.

8. The Resolution and Climax

The hero stood for the good of the innocent people that will be sacrificed in order for his father to take revenge. The hero destroyed his father. He then exact revenge on the king, too. The hero became the victor.

On the other hand, some games follow the Three Act structure. A good example of RPGs that uses the Three Act structure are Final Fantasy VII, Final Fantasy VIII, and Xenogears By the way, the eight sequences can be correlated to the Three Act Structure. Act I contains sequences 1 and 2. Act II contains sequences 3, 4, 5, and 6. And Act III contains sequences 7, and 8.

Aside from properly structuring your stories, you must include some common RPG story elements in your game. These elements will make it easy for your story to get digested by the players because they allow the players to somehow predict the story. A strong storyline has the following elements:

1. Introduction of the realm and the character

It is important to determine the character and the world that he is moving on at the beginning of the game. This is usually done by creating a narrative or a cutscene after the selection or creation of the character, which explains the character's traits and how the world around him works. By doing so, you can set the player's expectation of the character's skills and how he reacts to everything that he would encounter during the rest of the game.

2. Evolution of character

You can think that an RPG character is a zero-to-hero type of character — you often reveal that something great is going to happen to the character if the player progresses in the story. By setting that expectation, you need to create spaces in the story wherein the character levels up, acquires equipment and items that will improve or downgrade his skills, or encounters a scenario wherein the character would change into someone that is a step closer to the goal. The evolution of the character also adds to how the game builds up into an exciting adventure.

Most RPGs make characters vulnerable to pain, disease, and even death, and that adds up to the excitement of the game. By knowing that the character can be defeated by his enemies and the environment, the player becomes aware that the universe within the story is still more powerful than the character that he has created. In turn, the story forces the player to play within the restrictions of the game in order for him or her to progress.

3. Interaction with antagonists

An RPG game does not have to have a villain — the antagonist in the story can be the character's environment if you want it that way. However, the story builds up each time the playable character struggles against the antagonist, and when that happens, another section of the story unfolds. Antagonists also allow the player to realize that with the skills that are attached to the character come risks and rewards.

4. Quests

Instead of simply seeing that the character is in a higher level, players play quests that correspond to the available skills and traits of the character. The better the skills and the stats of the character, the harder the quest is going to be.

Quests would also allow you to gauge the logical abilities that the player has acquired during the duration of his gameplay. When you are aware that the player has learned to investigate, gather, or move efficiently during an easier quest, it makes sense for you to allow him to move to a different, more difficult quest.

5. Character abilities and actions

The storyline of the game allows the character abilities to improve in order to achieve the more difficult goals in the future. In an RPG, the player predicts the likelihood of the character becoming successful in achieving a series of goals based on the character's stats and range of abilities.

Depending on the allowable actions in a game, a player has a range of things to do in a game, but also makes him constantly responsible for the actions that he would take within the game. Since an RPG follows a real-life logic based on all possibilities available, the game also follows a particular set of emotions and morals. For example, games that allow players to steal or murder other characters may find themselves facing repercussions of their actions.

An RPG may also make it possible for the player to change his mind within the game about the set of abilities that he has set on the character that he has chosen, making him explore all the possible ways to achieve the end of the game. He may choose to later develop his character with a fusion of abilities that may not be available to him at the start of the game.

6. Items and Inventory

Items allow the character to improve his stats or to gain abilities within the game. It may also be necessary for the player to get a particular item that adds an event within the game to unlock a quest or a bonus. Like in most games, the rarer or more valuable the item, the harder it is to acquire.

Most RPG games exploit the use of limited inventory of the character in order to limit the possibilities available to the player when it comes to finishing a particular quest. It also makes the player decide which items are more important to him in order to address a particular in-story problem. By doing so, the game becomes more deductive.

Optional: Purchases or Trades

Modern RPGs make full use of commerce to create rewards within the game. Progressing in the game by defeating enemies or finding treasures allows the character to collect gems or money that allows him to purchase from merchants.

However, some games also incorporate interaction with other characters or non-playable characters (NPC) in order to get an item. This is usually done by trading a particular item in exchange for another that he would not be able to secure within any other parts of a quest.

By incorporating all these elements within the story of the game, you would be able to create a solid storyline and a universe for your characters that follows strict logic. By making it logical to play, you would be able to make the players of your game understand your goals as a game maker and play according to how you have set the parameters of your video game.

Chapter 6: Making the Rules

Now that you are aware of all the elements of the storyline that you can use to make your game playable and enjoyable, it's time to establish the rules of the game. Follow these steps to make sure that you would be able to maintain the flow of the game with every player's chosen action.

1. Write the outline of the game.

Create a timeline of all the events that would be taking place in the story. Usually, this would be a list of all the chapters and subchapters in the game's story. By doing so, you would be able to envision what the story would look like from start to finish.

You should have been able to create this as of this moment. But as of now, just follow the sequences that you have written in your story. Forget about the unimportant side quests. It is much important to establish the backbone story of your RPG first.

On the other hand, this would also work like your game's to-do list, which also includes all the elements that you need to explain to the player in order for him or her to understand the rules of your game. This includes the objectives within the game, as well as stat upgrades and possible downgrades. Keep in mind that you need to do this as soon as you have a concept for your game to keep your work on track.

2. Create your character list.

After you know what is going to happen in the universe that you are going to create, start making your characters. Write down all the traits and abilities of your main character/s, major and minor antagonists, and the NPCs that you would be incorporating in your game. Since you are creating a homebrew project, you can use

34

Microsoft Office or Excel for this document. If you can also attach image pegs for these characters, do so.

At this point, keep in mind to make the characters varied but simple. Since you are aiming to create a game in a day, do not aim for a complex character creation yet, like done in Skyrim. Also, do not aim for multiple characters with different backstories, like what was done in all of the Final Fantasy franchises. For now, stick with a single main character and develop his or her stats and story. If you would later choose to expand your game, you can do so by adding other elements in your outline.

3. Create your map.

Here is a very simple but very effective model of creating the world map for your first game: Create dungeons, then the town, then the interior, and then the world. The dungeon (or forest or cave, depending on your concept), where most of the adventure (and the loot) comes from, creates a setting for tasks and makes it easier for you to create a story that the people in the town setting would talk about. It's like creating the problem for your character to solve first to make the story move forward. The town can be a static map on your game where some non-playable characters can appear to provide an atmosphere and missions for the character as the story progresses. The world map can also be adjusted at a later time, depending on how many dungeons you are planning to have.

You can create at least one dungeon concept, and then later choose to auto-generate your dungeon map using software. However, make sure that you think about the skills of the playable character as well. Depending on what the character has "learned" during the game, come the elements that would make your dungeons tricky. For example, if you have decided that your character will learn the skill High Jump in a previous level, then you may decide to place the exit of your next dungeon on a higher ground.

Most game developers say that a three-layer dungeon makes an RPG very enjoyable, since it sets the expectation that the character would encounter the level's boss at the innermost part of the game. A three-layer dungeon would also make the player test out the skills of his or her character and make use of the items that he or she has already found earlier in the game. With layered dungeons, you make any RPG player find your game enjoyable by creating choices and making exploration possible.

4. Create the gameplay.

If you are trying to do an RPG wherein you would be hunting animals and pilfering villages to advance further in the game, decide whether this would appear onscreen as a 2D side scrolling adventure or if it would be a turn-based action for your players. You can later program the frequency of success and failure of actions that your player would choose, based on the stats of the character that he or she has chosen or created.

For now, keep the gameplay simple. Stick to one style for your first homebrew project — decide whether the actions would be displayed as a series of images with texts and action options, or simple movements without much regard to lifelike movements and rules. If you attempt to complicate the gameplay, you may end up making an extremely complex game that is unplayable for most players.

It would also make your life easier if you make the gameplay quantifiable, instead of using random rolls to decide the outcome of each action in the game. You can do this by thinking of a formula to determine the win or loss of a character during a specific quest.

5. Think of "if-then" scenarios.

Now that you know how the game would look like to the players, think of the actions and the consequences that will happen within the game. For example, if the player chooses the option of attacking a villager NPC to get the item there instead of picking his house when the NPC is not visible, you can add a rule that this would lead to imprisonment and loss of some gems that he had already gathered.

However, as a new RPG developer, it is best that you should stick with linear stories first. Adding multiple branches in your story is a difficult thing to do. And it is usually messy if the developers prioritize the branches first before the main story.

Giving your game multiple endings seems like a rad idea; however, be realistic. Many ambitious developers tend to put in all their ideas immediately in one game. And usually, they end up frustrated and their games were left unfinished.

6. Create your monsters.

Monsters are the minor characters in the game that create more possible logical choices in every RPG. For your first game, it is best to create at least four types of monsters that the main character/s would battle in every dungeon. You will find these classic monster types in many RPGs:

a. The Tank – They are often large and intimidating. They also can give and take a lot of pain to playable characters.

b. The Blocker – They are monsters that often take damage or heal a cluster of monsters. They can also create buffs against the player's party by dealing poison or stunning.

c. The Support – They are monsters that often have long-range powers and often support the tank.

d. The Irritating Ones – These monsters are used sparingly within games to add a twist to the range of monsters that a player may encounter. Most of the time, these monsters are slippery and may steal some items from the character. However, they give out huge bonuses when they are found and defeated.

Once you are able to develop your monsters, space them out in the map. Think that every 20 steps that the character would make would trigger a monster event, but there are some areas and paths that would not have monsters at all.

7. Create the battle rules.

Battle rules are the life of any RPG, and if you are going to revisit all the RPGs that you have played in the past, they all follow the rules of nature. For example, bows are effective against flying elements and ice always defeats fire. However, you can make your game slightly deviate from these classic rules by adding some twists in the battle guidelines within the game. For example, you can give the player a choice to use the Sing action to enrage any rhinoceros found in the map.

8. Create a reward/loss system.

In order to make the game more exciting and more motivating to play (or probably earn more money when you decide to sell it), create a reward/loss system based on the bonus items, damages dealt to antagonists, or any factor in the game that you can measure numerically. This system would also allow the player's character stats to improve or degrade, depending of course on the actions that he chooses to take.

For example, if the player chooses to trade a knife equipped for a broadsword, the character's attack power may improve, but it would make his speed decrease by a couple of notches.

9. Create an atmosphere.

The atmosphere of your setting is the soul of your RPG — without it, your game would feel empty and driven with no emotions, even when the character encounters more difficult tasks in the game. Most of the time, the atmosphere is driven by the combination of narratives, graphics, and sounds, and when mixed well during the programming process, they would create a great atmosphere that would translate into a better setting and a more enjoyable feel for the entire game. A good atmosphere also moves the story forward.

10. Think about endgame content.

The end of the game does not have to mean that the story is over for your audience, and you can use this cherry-on-top tactic to keep the audience hooked on your game even though they have finished the entire game already. By creating an intriguing endgame content, you make your audience look forward to your next creation or consider playing the game again.

11. Test the game.

Once you are done with all the elements, it's time to test the logic of the game. You can do this using paper first — you do not want to code something that may not work out fine. Ask someone to assume the role of a player and then implement the system that you have created. If the player successfully finishes all the dungeons and reaches the end of the storyline, then your game works!

Conclusion

Thank you again for purchasing this book!

I hope this book was able to help you to create your first role-playing game.

The next step is to find the idea development engine that you can use to create your next game and to launch it, too. Remember to be patient as you go about this endeavor and keep trying until you get it right — but also keep in mind that you don't have to go all-out on your first try. Stay relaxed, and most of all, have fun!

Finally, if you enjoyed this book, please take the time to share your thoughts and post a review on Amazon. It'd be greatly appreciated!

Thank you and good luck!

Check Out My Other Books

Below you'll find some of my other popular books that are popular on Amazon and Kindle as well. Simply click on the links below to check them out. Alternatively, you can visit my author page on Amazon to see other work done by me.

Android Programming in a Day

Python Programming in a Day

C Programming Success in a Day

C Programming Professional Made Easy

JavaScript Programming Made Easy

PHP Programming Professional Made Easy

C ++ Programming Success in a Day

Windows 8 Tips for Beginners

HTML Professional Programming Made Easy

If the links do not work, for whatever reason, you can simply search for these titles on the Amazon website to find them.

www.ingramcontent.com/pod-product-compliance
Lightning Source LLC
Chambersburg PA
CBHW071016180526
45168CB00003B/1444